MODERN ENGINEERING MARVELS

BIONIC EYES

Christine Zuchora-Walske

Checkerboard Library

An Imprint of Abdo Publishing
abdopublishing.com

ABDOPUBLISHING.COM

Published by Abdo Publishing, a division of ABDO, PO Box 398166, Minneapolis, Minnesota 55439.
Copyright © 2018 by Abdo Consulting Group, Inc. International copyrights reserved in all countries.
No part of this book may be reproduced in any form without written permission from the publisher.
Checkerboard Library™ is a trademark and logo of Abdo Publishing.

Printed in the United States of America, North Mankato, Minnesota
062017
092017

THIS BOOK CONTAINS
RECYCLED MATERIALS

Design: Kelly Doudna, Mighty Media, Inc.
Production: Mighty Media, Inc.
Editor: Liz Salzmann
Cover Photograph: Getty Images
Interior Photographs: Alamy, p. 25; AP Images, pp. 9, 13, 16, 17, 23, 27, 29 (top), 29 (bottom); Bryan
Jones/Flickr, p. 22; Getty Images, p. 1; iStockphoto, pp. 5, 11, 28 (top); Shutterstock, pp. 8, 12, 15
(left), 15 (right), 19, 21 (top left), 21 (top right), 21 (bottom left), 21 (bottom right), 26; Wikimedia
Commons, pp. 7, 20, 28 (bottom)

Publisher's Cataloging-in-Publication Data

Names: Zuchora-Walske, Christine, author.
Title: Bionic eyes / by Christine Zuchora-Walske.
Description: Minneapolis, MN : Abdo Publishing, 2018. | Series: Modern
    engineering marvels.
Identifiers: LCCN 2016962791 | ISBN 9781532110887 (lib. bdg.) |
    ISBN 9781680788730 (ebook)
Subjects: LCSH: Bioengineering--Juvenile literature. | Biomedical engineering--
    Juvenile literature. | Technological innovations--Juvenile literature. |
    Inventions--Juvenile literature.
Classification: DDC 620--dc23
LC record available at http://lccn.loc.gov/2016962791

CONTENTS

BIONIC EYES OF THE FUTURE

"It's 6:00 a.m. It's 6:00 a.m." Your talking alarm clock wakes you up. You feel for the off button and press it. Then you roll out of bed and get ready for school.

Even though you're blind, you can walk around your home quickly and easily. Everything's always in the same place. But away from home, you walk slowly, holding a long, white cane. With it, you feel for objects around you.

When the school bus arrives, you find the bus steps with your cane and climb aboard. As you ride, you think about a new **technology** your parents told you about. It's an **implant** that could help blind people see. You daydream about what that might be like.

One year later, you've had the implant surgery. Now you wear glasses. Your glasses hold a tiny camera and computer. The computer turns the camera's images into electronic signals. It sends the signals to a computer chip attached to your brain.

In 2014, there were nearly 300 million visually impaired people around the world.

Your brain reads the signals and lets you know what is around you. You can see! The shapes you see are kind of fuzzy. Everything looks black and white. But you don't need your cane anymore. You can see well enough to walk without it.

A world where blind people can see may seem far-fetched. But **bionic** eyes already exist. Their invention is the latest step in a long journey of discovery. That journey began centuries ago.

Benjamin Franklin lived in the 1700s. He was one of the founders of the United States. Franklin was also a scientist. He wanted to know more about electricity. In the 1750s, Franklin did many experiments with electricity.

Franklin and other scientists explored electricity throughout the late 1700s and the 1800s. They studied how it affects humans. They applied electricity to various body parts. Scientists used electricity to treat everything from toothaches to sore throats.

In 1874, scientists started electrifying living human brains to try to cure various illnesses. The first to do this was US scientist Roberts Bartholow. Then, in 1918, two German surgeons **stimulated** a patient's **visual cortex** with electricity. The electricity made the patient see dots of light called phosphenes.

Franklin's experiments with electricity led him to invent the lightning rod.

Scientists eventually experimented with using electricity to aid vision. In 1956, Australian scientist Graham Tassicker had an idea for a device that could be attached to a blind person's **retina**. The device contained a chemical that is sensitive to light. He believed the **implant** would allow a blind patient to see light. He patented his device but never tested it on a human.

In the 1960s and 1970s, British doctor Giles Brindley and US scientist William Dobelle did brain experiments. They attached **electrodes** to blind patients' **visual cortexes**. This caused specific patterns of phosphenes. The patients were able to identify the patterns.

These experiments offered hope for blind people. But the devices weren't practical.

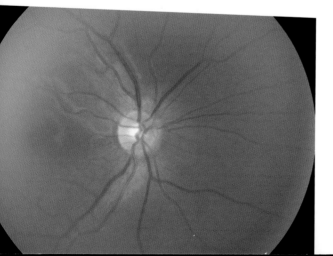

Blood vessels carry oxygen and nutrients to the retina. Like fingerprints, each person's retinal blood vessels have a unique pattern.

William Dobelle (*right*) continued to work on devices for blind people. In 2000, a blind patient, Jerry (*center*), received a brain implant developed by Dobelle.

At the time, computers and other electronics were big. They used a lot of wires and cables. The devices couldn't be carried around easily. So, blind people had to keep waiting for more advancements.

While some scientists did vision experiments, others were improving computers. Early computers were huge. They were powered by **vacuum tubes** linked by electrical wires. A computer could have thousands of vacuum tubes. They could fill a room!

A big step forward came in 1958. That year, US scientist Jack Kilby invented a device called an **integrated circuit (IC)**. Another US scientist, Robert Noyce, improved on Kilby's design a few months later. The IC was a thumbnail-size computer chip. It had tiny switches and thin metal pathways. One IC could do the same work as thousands of vacuum tubes and wires.

Thanks to the IC, computers became smaller and more reliable. These changes made new **technologies** possible. Engineers started developing small, powerful electronic devices.

One of these devices was the **cochlear implant**. It was developed in the 1970s and 1980s. A cochlear implant helps **deaf** people hear. It has an external part with a microphone, a tiny computer, and a transmitter. The microphone senses

More than 300,000 cochlear implants have been registered worldwide.

sounds. The computer turns the sounds into electrical signals. The transmitter sends the signals through a wire to **electrodes**. The electrodes are attached to the **cochlea** inside the ear. The cochlea passes the signals to the brain. This lets the person hear the sounds.

Cochlear implants have been quite successful. They have become a common treatment for **deafness**. Scientists hoped to build on cochlear implant **technology** to develop devices to restore vision to blind people.

At first, these developers focused on helping visually **impaired** people read. But during the 1980s, audio recordings of books became popular. By the 1990s, reading was a less important goal.

Over time, computers kept getting smaller and smaller. They became much easier to carry around. Then, in the early 2000s, engineers linked a tiny **portable** camera and computer to **electrodes**. This turned images into electrical signals.

Scientists believed this technology could be used in **bionic**

TECH TIDBIT

ENIAC was one of the first computers that could be programmed to do many kinds of tasks. It was completed in 1946 and weighed more than 30 tons (27 t)!

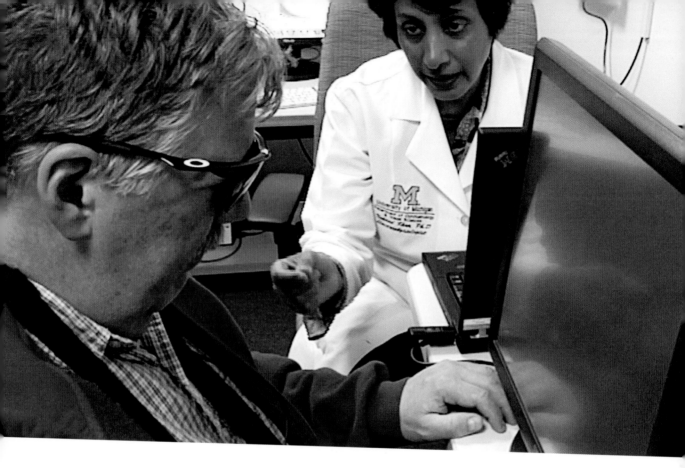

Roger Pontz (*left*) works with Dr. Naheed Khan (*right*) to test his vision after receiving a bionic eye.

eyes to improve the **mobility** of blind people. They started developing two different kinds of bionic eyes. One is an eye **implant**. The other is a brain implant. Each kind helps people with different kinds of vision problems.

EYE IMPLANTS

The eyes and brain work together to help a person see. The eyes' lenses focus light and images onto the **retinas**. The retinas contain cells called rods and cones. These cells convert light into electrical signals. The signals travel along the optic nerves to the brain. Then the brain tells the person what the images are. Damage to one or more of these parts can cause blindness.

Eye **implants** can help people who have damaged retinas but working optic nerves. Doctors can place **electrodes** in or on the retina or on the optic nerves. The person wears glasses fitted with a tiny camera. The camera records images. It sends the images to a small computer the person is carrying.

The computer turns the images into electronic signals. It sends the signals to the electrodes. The electrodes send the signals along the optic nerves to the brain. The brain decodes the signals. It tells the person what the images are.

One eye implant, called the Argus II, is already on the market in Europe and the United States. It was invented in California

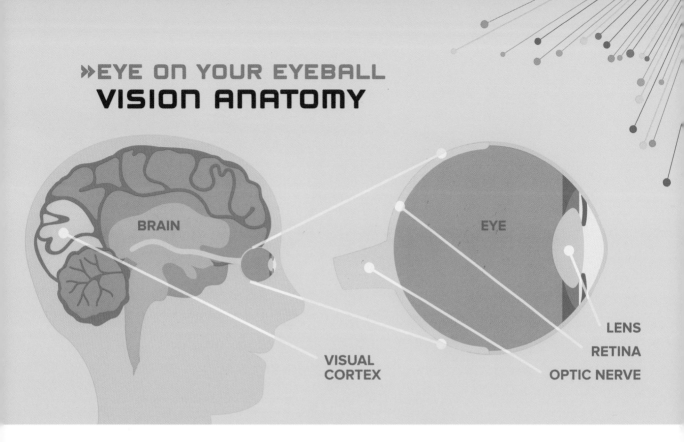

▶EYE ON YOUR EYEBALL
VISION ANATOMY

BRAIN

EYE

VISUAL
CORTEX

LENS

RETINA

OPTIC NERVE

by scientist and professor Mark Humayun. Humayun started working on an eye **implant** in the early 2000s.

Between 2002 and 2004, Humayun tested an early version of the implant, called the Argus I. The Argus I implant used 16 **electrodes**. During testing, several people received the Argus I. With the implant, these patients were able to tell the difference between light and dark objects.

The Argus retinal implants were designed for patients suffering from retinitis pigmentosa. This disease causes the rods and cones in the retinas to break down.

Humayun then developed the Argus II. It was similar to the Argus I, but it had 60 **electrodes**. In 2007, he began testing the Argus II in people. The patients who received the **implant** could recognize motion and see basic shapes.

⟫TECH TITAN
MARK HUMAYUN

Mark Humayun was born in Pakistan in the 1960s. He grew up in the United States after his family moved there in 1972. Humayun eventually went to medical school. During that time, his grandmother went blind from **diabetes**. Humayun decided that he would devote his life to studying blindness and helping blind people see.

Humayun became an **ophthalmologist** and an engineer. He teaches both medicine and engineering at the University of Southern California in Los Angeles. In 2013, the Argus II became the first bionic eye implant approved for US use.

US President Barack Obama (*right*) awarded Humayun the National Medal of Technology and Innovation in 2016.

In 2011, the Argus II was approved for use in Europe. And in 2013, the **Food and Drug Administration (FDA)** approved the Argus II for use in the United States. More than 200 people are already using the Argus II. Humayun plans to continue improving his **bionic** eye **implants**. Other **retinal** implants are also being developed. These include the IRIS II bionic vision system by French company Pixium Vision.

7 BRAIN IMPLANTS

Brain **implants** are for people who were once able to see but whose optic nerves became damaged. So, their eyes work fine, but their brains don't receive information from their eyes. A brain implant could solve this problem. No implants are approved for use right now. But a team of scientists at Monash University in Australia is leading the effort to develop a brain implant.

In 2009, Monash University joined forces with several companies to develop a brain implant. The companies involved include **technology** company Grey Innovation and medical engineering company MiniFAB. Together, they formed the Monash Vision Group (MVG).

The MVG brain implants use some of the same basic parts as the devices of the 1960s. These include a computer and **electrodes**. But the parts are smaller and more powerful. Tiny electronic cameras are also now available. And inserting a wire through the skull is no longer necessary. The implants can use a wireless connection.

The Monash Vision Group is located on the Clayton, Australia, campus of Monash University.

To attach the **implant**, surgeons remove a small piece of the patient's skull. They place several tiny tiles on the patient's **visual cortex**. Each tile has 43 **electrodes**. Then the surgeons replace the removed skull piece with a special cover. Then the patient wears glasses fitted with a camera and computer. These send information to the electrodes through a wireless connection.

The Monash team believes that patients who test this device will see visual patterns formed from hundreds of phosphenes. Patients should be able to see nearby people and objects. This will allow them to find their way around, both outdoors and indoors. MVG plans to begin testing the implant in humans in 2017.

The patients testing the Monash implants will receive them at the Alfred Hospital in Melbourne, Australia.

VISION IMPLANTS

TRANSMITTER:
A transmitter sends the computer's signals wirelessly to the **electrodes**.

COMPUTER
A computer turns the camera's images into electronic signals.

CAMERA
A camera gathers images from the surroundings.

OPTIC NERVE
The optic nerve carries signals from the **retina** to the brain.

VISUAL CORTEX
The **visual cortex** is the brain area responsible for decoding visual signals.

ELECTRODES
One or more MEAs receive the signals and send them to the brain.

RETINA
The retina is a layer of light-sensitive nerve cells that turns images into electrical signals.

21

Whether they are brain **implants** or eye implants, **bionic eyes** can greatly improve a person's quality of life. They allow people who are visually **impaired** to see again, or see better. Users of the Argus II say how happy they are to have more independence. Best of all, they can see their loved ones.

But the bionic eyes currently available have their limits. Users can see the **contrast** between light and dark areas and the edges of objects. But they can't see clearly. They can only see in black and white. And the images are blurrier than scientists expected. Most users are still unable to read.

Argus II users are technically blind. The best vision they get is about 20/1,000. That means they see at 20 feet (6 m) what a person with normal vision sees at 1,000 feet (305 m).

TECH TIDBIT

An implant uses a device called a multielectrode array (MEA). An MEA is a tiny grid with many **electrodes**.

After bionic eye surgery, the patient undergoes intensive therapy to learn how to process and understand images.

Another problem is that the Argus II costs more than $100,000. The surgery to **implant** it is also expensive. And like all surgeries, it is risky. But both scientists and patients continue to hope for better results from the next generation of **bionic** eyes.

Despite the drawbacks, there is encouraging news about **bionic** eyes. Engineers are working hard to improve bionic eyes. In particular, Second Sight, the company that makes the Argus II bionic eye, is planning some big upgrades.

The next version of Argus II will let users see colors. It will provide sharper vision. Users will be able to adjust their eyesight. They will be able to fine-tune focus and brightness.

Other scientists are developing amazing new ideas for restoring vision. One of these ideas is optogenetics. Optogenetics is the process of using light to control living nerve cells. Scientists insert proteins into the surviving **retina** cells to make them more sensitive to light. This process works best for people whose retinas are damaged but not destroyed. It could help people see with their own eyes instead of an **implant**.

A group of scientists in Germany is working on an alternative to mounting cameras on eyeglasses. They are developing a camera-like sensor that's built into a retinal implant. This type of

Raymond Flynn was the first patient with macular degeneration to receive a bionic eye. Macular degeneration is the most common cause of sight loss in the world.

implant would be for people who have working optic nerves. It is called the Alpha IMS.

Some scientists are dreaming really big. They are working on **bionic** eyes that can sense more than just **visible light**. With these eyes, people could see infrared radiation, or heat. They could see **ultraviolet** light. They might even have **X-ray** vision or be able to see certain gases!

Scientists and engineers constantly experiment with and develop new **technologies**. And they keep learning more about how the eyes and brain work. It seems possible that these efforts could eventually completely cure blindness!

TECH TIDBIT

Even people with perfect vision can't see ultraviolet light. But some insects, such as bumblebees, can.

Humans aren't the only ones with bionic eyes! Veterinary ophthalmologists have tested retinal implants on cats with retinal diseases causing blindness.

TECH TIMELINE

1918
Two German surgeons stimulate a patient's visual cortex with electricity.

1958
Jack Kilby and Robert Noyce invent the integrated circuit (IC).

1970s–1980s
Scientists develop the cochlear implant, which is very successful.

1750s
Benjamin Franklin experiments with electricity.

1956
Graham Tassicker invents an implant that could allow a blind person to see light.

1960s–1970s
Giles Brindley and William Dobelle stimulate blind people's visual cortexes.

EARLY 2000s

Engineers link a tiny portable camera and computer with electrodes and turn real-world sights into electrical signals.

2016

Monash University scientists begin testing their brain implant in humans.

2007

Mark Humayun begins testing the Argus II in humans.

GLOSSARY

bionic–using electronic devices to assist with normal human body functions.

cochlea–a hollow tube in the inner ear. Something related to the cochlea is cochlear.

contrast–noticeable differences.

deafness–a condition in which someone is wholly or partly unable to hear. A person with this condition is deaf.

diabetes–a disease in which the body cannot properly absorb normal amounts of sugar and starch.

electrode–a point through which electricity flows in or out of a device or substance.

Food and Drug Administration (FDA)–a government agency that monitors food and drug safety.

impaired–having a defective physical or mental function.

implant–to put a device inside the body using surgery. Such a device is called an implant.

integrated circuit (IC)–a set of electronic circuits on a small chip.

mobility–the ability to move.

ophthalmologist (ahf-thuhl-MAH-luh-jihst)–a doctor who deals with the structure, functions, and diseases of the eye.

portable–able to be carried easily.

retina–the lining at the back of the eyeball that sends images to a person's brain. Something related to the retina is retinal.

stimulate –to excite to activity or growth or to greater activity.

technology– a capability given by the practical application of knowledge.

ultraviolet–relating to a type of light that cannot be seen with the human eye.

vacuum tube–a tube that is a near-vacuum through which an electrical current can pass.

visible light–light that can be seen by the human eye.

visual cortex–the part of the brain that processes visual information.

X-ray–a photograph taken by rays that can pass through substances that light cannot.

WEBSITES

To learn more about Modern Engineering Marvels, visit **abdobooklinks.com**. These links are routinely monitored and updated to provide the most current information available.

INDEX